Part of the Darkness

PART OF THE DARKNESS

Poems

David J. Rothman

ENTASIS PRESS
WASHINGTON, D.C.

Published by

ENTASIS PRESS

WASHINGTON, D.C.

2013

ISBN 978-0-9850997-1-8

Library of Congress Control Number: 2012955117

Cover art by V. Lowe: *Tangent XI*
Conte crayon on paper, 8 inches x 8 inches, 2012

For Roseanne S. Soffer (1921-1996)
"Suffer, with an *o."*

Contents

I. AT THE RUINED TEMPLE

II. HYDROGEN BOMB IGNITION SEQUENCE

III. KISSING FOR CYNICS

IV. Bring It

Part of the Darkness

Ich bin ein Theil des Theils, der Anfangs alles war,
Ein Theil der Finsterniß, die sich das Licht gebar...
        Mephistopheles
        Faust, Erster Teil
        Johann Wolfgang von Goethe

But I'm part of the Part which at the first was all,
Part of the Darkness that gave birth to Light...
        George Madison Priest, translator

I. AT THE RUINED TEMPLE

At the Ruined Temple

Older, wiser, more knowing and now sad,
Let us marvel at confidence and joy,
Marvel at the long-extinguished boy
Who woke each day and all at once was glad.
Where is he now? Why are some nights so bad?
How did time earn the power to destroy?
Who hauled the awful horse up into Troy?
For now his smoldering mid-life world's gone mad:
Here comes our man, Anchises on his shoulder.
Ascanius holds his hand, Creüsa's dead.
He flees his conquered youth, its silent names.
Ceres' ruined temple feels far colder.
There's sorrow here and more hard times ahead.
Silent, he watches the city go up in flames.

To Go

She laughed at me again and said "Give up."
Lovely in that Maxfield Parrish dress.
Ringlets. Blue eyes. "You know you can't live up
To it, yourself, the past, or…You're a mess."
I gazed at her. She shrugged, took one last bite
Of pear then tossed the core off in the grass.
"But…" I said, and she said "Let's not fight.
Really. You're a royal pain in the ass."
I started scribbling. "What are you doing now?"
"Just vulgar fragments," and I offered some.
Propped on one elbow, furrow on her brow,
She rolled her eyes, said "Man, you're so damn dumb."
"Not yet," I said. "You want this wine to go?"
She grabbed her keys, stood up and told me: "No."

Matins

If God could see us now maybe he'd say
Something gentle, something true and wise.
Perhaps explain why he had gone away.
Who knows? He might even apologize.
So let's imagine buying God a beer,
Prepared to listen, though we have a list:
Hate love light darkness sadness glory fear.
First chance we get, we smile. "You've been missed,"
We say, but things just go downhill from there.
He throws his head back, roars with laughter, farts,
Starts telling filthy jokes, flies through the air
Singing "I'm gonna kick…your ass…at darts."
Then he starts to cry and kills a child.
We cower. His cold eyes burn with sweetness wild.

Arrival

I was lost in thought when he arrived
Through that picture window like a star,
Or maybe just starlight. He sang. I strived
To ignore his melodies, that thin, red scar —
But he's quite patient. Walked around. Returned
In one of my good sweaters. I stayed calm.
He pulled and thumbed through books from which I'd learned
To recognize him and his angry psalm.
"Well," he said looking up, "I notice none
Of these tomes bears your name upon the spine."
"No," I said, "not yet." He laughed. What fun
For him. "Face facts," he said. I said, "Let's dine."
He told me, "Well, I have some time to kill...
Alright." He flayed a lamb. I lit the grill.

Acting My Age

Black clouds were sparking up the sky when I
Gave up. I'd wanted spells, some palindrome
That would dissolve us both like smoke or foam
Into one element, freeing the eye.
Then, I believed, our lives would meet, defy
Their own defining fractals and become
Each other's air and fire, sea and loam —
We'd build a lovers' bed from earth and sky.
But words don't fit the tune of that lullaby.
Words bark, alive and feral. They hunt and roam
Like animals beneath the sparkling dome
Of rhetoric, doing what they deny.
So I put my pen down, tore up this page,
And thought of getting a job. Acting my age.

This Bright Edge

"No problem!" She raised her radiant hand and struck
Me smack down back down in the frozen mud.
Oh wonderful, great, this is just my luck,
My own guardian angel out for blood.
"Not bad, considering you don't exist,"
I said, and tried to get back on my feet.
"Not so fast," she said and grabbed my wrist,
Then hurled me through a cloud of driving sleet.
Popped out the other side. The air thin, quiet.
Blue fading up to black. Apex. I floated.
So far away. Here no mistakes, no riot
Of love, no heart with which to be devoted.
Landed with a crash in someone's hedge.
The vision? Gone. Her answer: this bright edge.

We All Got Up to Dance

None of us stood the slightest chance.
There was nothing left to do.
We all got up to dance.

Someone proclaimed the end of romance.
She said the time for love was through.
None of us stood the slightest chance.

Someone got drunk and took off his pants.
Some of us cheered. Some decided to sue.
We all got up to dance.

Someone talked himself into a trance,
Proclaiming he knew what God knew.
None of us stood the slightest chance.

Someone got paid a fat advance
For denying anything was true.
We all got up to dance.

Since then, baby, I've had to go freelance.
You have to do what you have to do.
None of us stands the slightest chance,
So come on, sweetheart — let's get up and dance.

As for Myself

As for myself — well, in the end, who cares?
A million cars course freeways in the sun.
In Kashgar, a knife-man offers up his wares.
The fat boy breaks a chair, demanding fun.
As for myself — I'll be whatever you wish.
The cat has left a mouse head at the door.
The madam's cooking for the girls: fresh fish.
Beneath all theories stand the curious poor.
As for myself — I heard a song somewhere
About how certain things cannot be told.
I drink to that and plan to drink my share.
At dusk the mountain's shadow grows so cold.
As for myself — what difference does it make?
Look: the stars, the pines, the deep, dark lake.

II. Hydrogen Bomb Ignition Sequence

Let It Snow

Let it snow. Let blue skies fade to steel.
Let wind gust, then pick up, flat light creep in.
Let clouds arrive, pile up, grow dark, conceal.
Let weathermen issue a bulletin.
Let the first flakes fall like the kiss in a seduction,
Full of promise, tenderness, and danger.
Let them whisper imminent destruction,
Then unfurl their fiery love and anger.
Let darkness fall, let freedom freeze, let things
Break down berserk, dark spirals bust out big,
And flake on flailing flake sculpt thickening rings
Of drifts beyond what any plow can dig.
The ground is bare, the flowers dead. Let's go:
It's winter, time for blizzards. Let it snow.

That Apple

As for the fruit, it had no taste at all.   Donald Justice

The angel pointed. Giant wings unfurled.
We approached the open gate with heavy tread.
Before us lay a wilderness, the world,
Where we knew we would one day name the dead.
"Hey Gabe, one thing that's on my mind," said Eve.
"What are you, nuts?!" I said, "Shut up! Let's go!
He's armed and angry. Honey, let's just leave."
"Cut it out," she said. "Hey Gabe! You know,
Adam lied. That apple was the best,
Sweet, ripe, ruby red and satisfying.
Its juice ran down my chin onto my breast,
And drinking it, I'm unafraid of dying."
Ooh, I love that woman. The angel roared.
"Well," I said, "at least we won't be bored."

Details

Enjoy the things you can. I'll be the fly
Caught in your honey, swimming in your soup.
I'll be the hitch, glitch, hook, lash in your eye,
The catch there always is, snag, last high hoop.
I'll be the pawn that's just one move behind
Or lonesome chromosome now off the track,
The short escape clause that you failed to find
Or tiny floating flake of brittle plaque.
I'm down here in the fine print, slow and steady,
A bolt two threads too short on a propeller,
A splinter, microorganism ready
To grow into your bloodstream's storyteller.
Go on, puff out your vast and hopeful sails.
I'll just keep working on the small details.

Dark Quantum Foam's Hereafter

Step back. That's you, friend, sitting in your chair.
Again — your home, your family, your car.
Once more. The city sparkles. Go on, stare.
The things you see are merely things that are.
And now the planet, half blue, brown and white,
The other half a region of deep needing,
Work, sleep, love, dinner, card games, death, delight —
Hey look, down there, there's even someone reading.
There goes the moon, next Mars, Jupiter, Saturn.
Now, voyager, the sun recedes into a cloud,
Cloud into spiral, spiral into pattern,
Pattern onto cloth draped like a shroud
Of storms upon dark quantum foam's hereafter.
And what's that sound…I can't tell…tears? Or laughter?

I Wash My Hands

We wash our hands by habit, wash them clean,
We wash no matter what we may believe.
The whole world understands it's good hygiene.
Now dry them, check the mirror, straighten, leave…
Even fools know that's how you behave.
Even criminals reach out for soap.
They wash their hands, the tyrant and sex-slave,
The teacher, butcher, senator, brain, dope.
So why is it sometimes so hard to do it
When we most need to rinse the past away?
I ought to wash my hands now that I'm through it,
It's time to let that memory go gray.
Yet in my dream I spin the faucet. Winter.
Frozen pipes. Deep in my palm, a splinter.

The Question

"Doc," I said, "it's so confusing now.
My life…my family…I can't make sense…"
He stopped, looked up, all ears, a furrowed brow.
I went on. Had to. The pressure so immense,
Words spilling out. "I mean, I'm 46,
And all my dreams, I don't…" Took a deep breath.
No good. Began to cry. "I just can't fix…"
Sob, "…anything, and so afraid of death…
So many things I never meant to say…
Mistakes, I mean…and all the loneliness…"
Regained control and tried to laugh. "Hey,
Not to mention the world's a total mess…"
X-rays in hand, puzzled, he said "I see.
But aren't you here to talk about your knee?"

Hair of the Dog

"News got you down again?" my old friend said,
As he slid into the booth across from me.
The local café. Breakfast. Fresh-baked bread,
Bacon and eggs, good coffee, refills free.
And spilling like cold blood out of the *Times*,
Today's glut of articulate ugliness —
The clichéd round of triggers, sighs and dimes —
A planet's accusations and distress.
He shrugs, reaches and plucks a sorry grape.
"You know," he says, pausing to chew and swallow,
"It's just a matter of time. There's no escape."
He smiles. A dog-eared deck fills his hand's hollow.
He says "The cold, dark house will always win.
Surely…" "Shut up," I say, "just deal me in."

Never Forgive

"Don't even think about it," his voice said.
I don't know how he got here in the shower.
"Admit you'd like to hear that guy is dead,
That hope was useless in his final hour."
Shampoo began to run into my eye.
A calm hand wiped my forehead with its thumb.
"Come on," he said, "You'd even watch him die.
You've done it in your dreams. So don't act dumb."
"And why not?" he went on. "He treated you
Like dirt. You needed help – he didn't answer.
He claimed to be your friend but was untrue.
Rejoice, be glad to learn of his quick cancer."
Then suddenly I was alone again,
With all the fear, the anger and the pain.

Moving Back to a Mountain Town

The truck has come and gone, the men are paid.
Our good old friends are glad to see us back.
Mount Emmons throws familiar evening shade.
White Rastas burn one down in the Friendship Shack.
Cardboard boxes fill the living room,
The boys have found their toys, play in the yard.
August flowers offer one last bloom —
The autumn frosts up here come soon and hard.
Night. Coyotes howl across the valley,
Exulting over what the pack has killed.
I stroll home down a funky, gravel alley
And ponder aspirations unfulfilled.
My youth is gone, long gone. Am I a fool?
I hear the cataract. I know the rule.

Are You Lucky?

"I know you'd like to say you beat the odds,"
The dealer said, now looking past my shoulder.
"So keep pretending you're loved by the gods.
Let dreams of luck persist as you grow older.
Take those hard-earned dollars out and plunk
Them dreaming down on one more lottery ticket.
Take up your work, pretend again the drunk
Dice of the universe will find and pick it.
Or…take my advice and save your nickel.
Say nothing, lay no plans, give up the hope
Vocation calls or love is more than fickle.
Any greater stake and you're time's dope."
He put his hand on mine. Cold grip and true.
I shook it off. He looked perplexed. No clue.
"It's not a peace sign, asshole. I'll take two."

You Can't Dance to the News

You can't do the twist to a suicide bomb,
And who wants to waltz in a dead girl's shoes.
You don't dosido while morticians embalm,
Folks, you just can't dance to the news.

You can't shuffle or tap on a tidal wave,
Or foxtrot across today's Waterloos.
Some have been known to dance on a grave,
But you just can't dance to the news.

No, you can't boogie down to the rockets' red glare,
Or krump in a war zone's ICUs.
Nobody rumbas bombs bursting in air,
I say you just can't dance to the news.

Ballet is lovely, but not on the bench.
The poor don't gavotte to the IMF's IOU's.
You can't saraband across battlefield stench.
No, you just can't dance to the news.

Let's go to a club, come on, you say,
But sweetheart I can't, I've got the blues.
I'm all shook up by what happened today —
Oh, I just can't dance to the news.

On the Human Condition

Obsessive and neurotic behavior is the price we pay for our
rapid cognitive evolution.   Robert G. Bednarik

"You really want to know?" he said. "It's sweet.
These two guys hatched a plan to rob some swell.
They had no money, not enough to eat,
Felt their lives sucked, so figured what the hell.
Out on parole, they thought they knew the ropes.
They'd break in, get the goods, leave, leave no trace.
The beauty of it was they were such dopes,
Followed this lady home to case the place,
I mean, if you want stuff you don't want folks
At home, but in they go. Look, Dad is sleeping
On the porch sheltered by tall, stately oaks
That don't mean shit, as don't the willows, weeping.
They beat him with a bat and tie him to
His bed and tape his mouth. But they're not through.

"They bind the girls and wife and take what cash
There is, then find this checkbook. What good luck!
It's morning now, new plan: a desperate dash
With mom downtown at gunpoint. 'If you fuck
Up, your family's dead,' he says. She gets
The cash but whispers to the teller why she's there.
Small town, slow cops, and now, my friend, all bets
Are off. Back home, the other guy goes where
Suggestion leads and rapes the little girl.
When his accomplice gets back with the dough
The other taunts him: 'Come on…take a whirl.'
And so he rapes the mother. Down below
The father wriggles free, escapes, hops, crawls
To a neighbor's. The cops close in too late, the walls

"Ignite, the mother strangled and each daughter,
Doused in gasoline, bound, smeared with semen,
Burns to death." He laughed. "Now, say how water,
O poet, or bright love could show the demon
What might be more sufficient to this day,
This day I own, this day that I have yearned
To give you so that I can hear you say
That you cannot forget what you have learned."
Then, broken, on my hands and knees, I said
"O demon, here I am, on black bedrock,
Your graven, bench-mark image in my head
My own. I yield. You win. But I have…" "Talk,"
He said. "…just one question. Can you explain
The cause of this inviolable pain?"

Another Day of Drowning

"First in the moment then out: it's hard to stay.
The wind is always fair and yet you come
About so quickly, turn and sail away
Into yourself, that past where you came from,
Not where and who you are and need to be.
Half-blind and flawed you tack that way then this,
As if some smart new course could set you free,
As if not being present gives you that."
"Captain," I said, "Nice try. But you're about
As Zen as a machine-gun firing blanks.
You'd trick me out of thought and thereby doubt,
Without which even you cannot give thanks.
But without 'If' there cannot be a 'Then.'"
"Good, good," the demon hissed. Gave me his pen.

Youth

I'm wiser now. So what? It's like the rack.
I loved my stupid youth, its limber luck.
I want my perfect love and anger back.

Each day was like a bone that I could crack,
Each night a ripe fruit I could bite and suck.
I'm wiser now. So what? It's like the rack.

Give me green dreams, blue dreams, in my dark shack.
Give me another chance to run amok.
I want my perfect love and anger back.

It's true the world gives in, breaks down, goes black,
And I acknowledge what the years will pluck:
I'm wiser now. So what? It's like the rack

To know the end of life's a stone-cold smack,
To know that even love can slow, get stuck.
I want my perfect love and anger back.

I'd be again a jacked-up Cadillac,
Lunatic, lover, poet, friend of Puck.
I'm wiser now. So what? It's like the rack.
I want my perfect love and anger back.

A Closer Walk with Thee

We strolled. He said, "I am your library.
Accept the names and learn the discipline
That any ear can hear or eye can see,
For that's the boundary you must live within.
I'm fossilized in every word you write,
I whisper inside everything you say.
I'm the future of the past, the night
And the nightmare, the daydream and the day.
And I don't turn, I only go and grow
Greater, real and unreal, less and more,
In a thousand tongues that you will never know.
I'm the map and what the map is for,
I'm words and dirt, a path both false and true."
"Well, yes," I said, "but I'm the other shoe."

Loyal Shadow

I'm every time you realized you were wrong.
I'm every well-intentioned dumb mistake.
I'm every moment that went on too long,
The apology that you just couldn't make.
I'm every clumsy gesture, stupid move,
The words you uttered better left unsaid.
I'm the point you thought you had to prove,
The hours wasted wrestling empty dread.
And more: I'm those times when they return
In your contrition, doubt, remorse and shame.
Delicious and invisible they burn,
Attached forever to your face and name.
Go where you wish, I'm your loyal shadow,
A growing gray-green cloud: your heart's tornado.

I I I I I

Arrogant soldiers always at salute,
Each growing like a tree without a root,
Your gates stand closed to every thought and sense,
Except what comes from your own present tense.
Your columns, although simplified and pure,
Sport capitals that lack a tablature,
Like what is left when everything's been stripped
From empty temples carved with long dead script.
You stride across the page in upper case
Insisting only you deserve this place,
Each kingless subject barking like a trumpet,
Informing every noun you're going to hump it.
"Let me out," you holler, stutter, stammer,
Yet you're the bars that hold you in your slammer,
A convict's smuggled chisel with no hammer.

Hey! You! Yeah, you! You! You, I mean you there.
You're all alone — why didn't you prepare?
Although you sound like one, you cannot see;
Although you look like one, you are not free.
You say your parts are far less than your sum,
But who can tell? For every part is numb.
Admit your little brother has a point:
No other letter offers you a joint.
Yes, all of your epistolary friends
Have other means and go to other ends,
While hopeful loves, whenever they come near,
Grow silent, thin, and then just disappear.
No, you don't want to rhyme. Why should you try?

For love obliges lovers to reply.
More perfect to insist and to deny,
Locked forever in a silent sigh.

Your business partners growl and grow irate,
For currency, to work, must circulate,
Which it cannot in your tight credit squeeze
That would refuse all externalities.
Yet even silver will begin to canker
If held forever by a selfish banker.
Each dollar wanders like an orphaned waif,
Starving in the kitchen of your safe.
Your blind ambition glitters like a jewel
Locked in the darkness by a midnight fool.

In short, you'd be a perfect narcissist
If you could only prove that you exist,
Which you can never do, for all creation
Can only reach its sum in conversation.
So, while there's no verb you can't conjugate,
Each time you do it you're already late,
Transforming every one into an it,
Through endless coils of sparkling, lively wit
In which the green world slowly starts to pale.
How sad that you can't crack just once, maybe fail.
But that's beyond your powers. Admit what's true:
That even you know you can't be a you.

Demon, Demon, What Do You See?

Darkness, darkness visible, smooth, quiet,
Pours from the stones, the mountains, rivers, oceans,
Drapes planets, caves, fens, bogs, eyes (why deny it?),
Fills buttons, windows, movies, nations, notions,
Moves every finger, passion, dollar, vow,
The arms of lovers, empties words, worlds, clocks,
Unmakes the verbs themselves, both then and now
And future, all that sings, swims, flies, walks, talks,
Is darkness, darkness, pain, abyss, desire,
Voracious interstellar black hole bang,
Rape's rapturous hateful void gone H-bomb fire,
Triumphant fear, all silence, thought, word, song,
Creation's pedal-point. Now do you understand?
"No," I said. "Look here. I hold it in my hand."

Free Advice

Everybody gets to be a person.
Everybody measures life in days.
Be grateful that you didn't get a worse one.
Enjoy your little piece of the malaise.
You're made from dirt that once came from a star
And nothing in creation should seem strange.
The way things are is just the way things are
And nothing you can do will make it change.
So when some nutcase goes and shoots a stranger,
Or bad luck twists your colon in a knot;
When love becomes inseparable from danger
And you learn every virtue can be bought;
Remember things could be far worse, far worse.
You see? I knew you could. And that's the curse.

Fire

When I was young I wanted only fire.
To smell smoke, taste it, feel heat, make life burn.
To know fire, eat it, be it, be its pyre,
To see it, breathe it, hear it, make it yearn
To spark, ignite, create, destroy, transform
My life to something great. The sacrifice?
Days, nights, words, water, calm noon, midnight storm,
The earth, the air, all pleasure and all vice.
But now, though flame still sparkles on my tongue
And cuts my eyes and fingers like a jewel,
I cannot pretend that I am young.
And I refuse to be a young fire's fool.
Peace and solace call. Slow honey drips.
Lover, taste that. Here. Here, on my lips.

Too Bad

Too bad I don't believe in anything —
It would be nice if life made fucking sense,
Suggesting words to say or songs to sing
Instead of merely offering events.
But, please…cool entropy's acetylene
Burns black beyond where anyone can see.
What you think is never what you mean:
No light escapes from this one certainty.
Things just happen or they don't, that's all.
Only fools or liars claim what's true.
Even matter doesn't matter. Small,
Always unraveling, it won't construe.
A shame. Some truth and beauty would have been alright.
Had it appeared, I might have even tried to write.

An Auction

Sweetheart, if it walks upon the earth,
Swims in the ocean or flies through the air,
It's for sale. No matter what it's worth,
Say, human life, yes, it's for sale somewhere.
And more: air, ocean, earth, you betcha, can
Be yours for a price, they're on this auction block,
Along with rights to do the things that man
Can do to them, down to the dark bedrock.
And why stop there? We market time, shares, debt,
Options, futures, war, philosophy.
We bet on things that don't exist as yet,
Then hedge, like a subjunctive prophecy.
Yes, darling, all the poems are for sale.
So — How much for the tongue of a nightingale?

Good Morning, America

*Egg, who are you, what are you, where did you come from
and where are you going?*   Carl Sandburg

Here's to learning's sunny optimism,
Relentless explanations of the magic.
Here's to compass, clock and syllogism,
Here's to Euclid, improver of the tragic.
Now let's drink to law, the judge's season,
To study, tank that trundles slowly on,
Till someone says…*and so this is the reason.*
Now, sweet child, the monsters all are gone.
Nice try. Not bad. But there's a little more.
The jealous woman kills her sons for spite.
The blind king staggers through his blood-stained door.
The general turned pawn puts out the light.
And fixed to your chair, powerful yet dumb,
Look: here is Gloucester's eye, here Cornwall's thumb.

Mandatory Entertainment

Spin until you're dizzy and spill your swill:
You'll make no escape from the shifting shapes
And Technicolor hex in this Tex-Mex airport bar
Where waiters distractedly take your time for a bill.
Walls crawl with unlikely icons and metaphors,
While eyes glaze with the traveler's isolation, tracking
False fullness that never fades back to black.
Drinkers swivel, stirring swizzle sticks as drivel drizzles
Everywhere. Sigh, try, and fail to stare nowhere,
For even the electron-drenched air fills with a glare
That is not there to the touch and offers no hatch
Back down away or out of this much much-too-much.
Thunder above, tarmac below, a full-on smack-talk heart attack here,
And there's no switch on this tiny apocalypse. No way to stop the show.

Your Name Here

Can you please tell me what this is about?
I didn't realize that it was so late.
You know I really want to help you out.
The other guy quoted a lower rate.
Just a bit can't hurt. I'll stop next week.
That is so interesting. Please tell me more.
Silence is golden. I choose not to speak.
I am so sorry to hear about his death.
The books are balanced and we're in the black.
This policy is going to help the poor.
In order to defend, we must attack.
Your name will cross my lips with my last breath.

"Of course not. Never. Never said you would.
And yet you seem to think that others could."

In Your Dreams

You've missed the boat. The train has left the station.
The machine is blinking, too bad you weren't here.
I'll pass your message on — he's on vacation.
The kitchen's closed. Sorry, we're out of beer.
The final bell has rung. The rules are set.
The doors are shut, the opera has begun.
Good tip, too bad you didn't place a bet.
The deadline passed last week. You're late. We're done.
Go ahead, cry, beg, fall to your knees,
Tears streaming down your face. The doctor's gone.
The milk is spilling to the floor. Say "Please,"
Be good, pray to your God and struggle on,
But you've lost out, you've lost your only chance,
And you look so absurd without your pants.

Since You Asked

"Are you OK?" they asked her, and she said,
Between her sobs, "Well, no, I'm not OK..."
But what did they expect? Her husband dead,
Their boy just three, another on the way,
Too many bills, his life, their life cut short
By one, two bullets in an Afghan field.
He dragged himself the length of a tennis court
Before he realized he would have to yield.
And there he bled to death, the boys, his friends,
Pinned down by gunfire until they called in
Some air support. And there that story ends.
Three dead. Just one of ours. A hard-fought win.
It has its logic, logic that holds sway.
But, since you asked? Well, no, she's not OK.

At His Brother's Grave

in memoriam, MHR, 1961 - 1998

What were you thinking, you god-damn stupid fuck?
What were you thinking? What is up with that?
I need an answer, Mike, because I'm stuck.

Couldn't you see that you'd run out of luck
One day and this is where you'd then be at?
What were you thinking, you god-damn stupid fuck?

Why couldn't you outgrow running amok,
You psychonarcedelic acrobat?
I need an answer, Mike, because I'm stuck,

Still stuck on how you had to go and chuck
Your one sweet life on junk's shit ziggurat.
What were you thinking, you narcissistic schmuck?

Why? For what? Did every day just suck
So much you needed dope's dark caveat?
I need an answer, Mike, because I'm stuck.

Here in the rain I'd love to be awestruck:
O brother, answer my magnificat:
What were you thinking, you god-damn stupid fuck?
I need an answer, brother. Oh, I'm stuck.

To the School Where I Was Once Headmaster

It's over now. The classrooms have gone dark.
Through the uncluttered hallways no one hollers.
Perhaps they'll tear it down and build a park.

And good for them — the thing's no great landmark.
The old front desk. Silent. No more callers.
It's over now. The library has gone dark.

They didn't even leave a question mark.
No more confusion, awakenings, stonewallers.
Perhaps they'll tear it down and build a park —

Not as good a place to hunt the snark,
But tough. I too admire our town's fastballers.
It's over now. The kitchen has gone dark,

The dorms are empty. It's time to disembark.
All hail the spec investment overhaulers.
Perhaps they'll tear it down and build a park.

So snap out of it! Recall the truth, the stark,
Relentless logic of the world's hard dollars.
It's over now. The whole place has gone dark.
Perhaps they'll tear it down and build a park.

Where Late the Sweet Birds Sang

The apples are all done.
Frost took those we didn't pick.
They shrivel in the sun.

November has begun.
Summer has played her last sweet trick.
The apples all are done.

Confused leaves overrun
The lawn. They swirl and billow thick
And shrivel in the sun.

The flies must know time's won.
Slow and weak they barely stick.
And the apples are all done.

The hunter fires his gun.
The buck is wounded to the quick.
His eyes shrivel in the sun.

Flowers? There are none.
In the wind the great clocks tick.
And the apples all are done.
They shrivel in the cold, cold sun.

Because

In those days everyone was always old.
If they said things were true, well, they were true.
When we were called we did what we were told.
We tried to do what we were told to do.
If there were things we didn't understand,
We didn't understand. A silence was
Just that. It seemed to us things could be planned,
Because, because, because, because, because.
I don't know when it changed and don't know how.
Perhaps it was the point at which I saw,
Across the field of pain that I know now
Cannot be mapped, for it transcends the law,
That once, when people said what they were going to do,
I'd thought, mistakenly, that such a thing was true.

Please Leave

O demon, please, I beg you, let me be.
Give me forgetfulness, indifference.
Leave my body and my memory.

Surely now's the time to set me free.
This love has gone beyond all common sense.
O demon, please, I beg you, let me be.

I would come to you on bended knee,
But my joints ache with sad experience.
Leave my body and my memory,

And if I call again, can we agree
That we should both engage in abstinence?
O demon, please, I beg you, let me be,

Release me in this year of Jubilee,
Let me forget your sweet magnificence.
Leave my body and my memory.

Just one thing — tell me — why must you be me?
I had no inkling of such violence.
O demon, please, I beg you, let me be.
Leave my body and my memory.

What Is This, Some Kind of Joke?

After work, the horse and mushroom crash
At the Oasis. Everyone is there —
The frog who's grown a man on his butt talks trash
With the potato, grasshopper and bear
Who ate the bar bitch, while the dancing duck
And seal admire the dog who licks his balls
Eternally. The five spot, short on luck,
Scribbles his number on the rest room walls.
What a bunch of clowns: the man who drinks
Until the photo of his wife looks good;
The genie going deaf who swears he thinks
The guy said "12-inch pianist;" the hood,
The penguin, the amnesiac, the flea.
The barkeep nods and pours a pint for me.

If You Want To Make God Laugh

Tell him your plans. Tell him the one about
That race you're going to win, that girl you know,
That pitch you'll use to strike each batter out,
Your scores, that college where you hope to go.
Inform him how you have prepared to keep
Your health, your looks, your temper and your money.
Advise him of your plans for deep, sweet sleep,
For satisfying work and love like honey.
And why stop there? Acquaint him with this town,
Its politics, hypocrisy, blacklists,
And how your leadership will shut that down.
Tell him you plan to prove that he exists.
Come on, speak up. Cat got your tongue? There's so much more.
But maybe you should stop. He's rolling on the floor.

On First Looking into a Trendy Literary Periodical

Much have I traveled in the realms of lead —
After all, I got a PhD —
And I have seen my share of idiocy,
Which made me want to go straight home to bed.
I generally like poets who are dead,
But when this magazine showed up for free
I figured why not, let's have a quick look-see,
You never know, don't be afraid to tread.
What a mistake. I've been annoyed all day.
I feel as though I ate a cosmic fart.
It's like one of those dreams: you've lost your way
On some dark street in the Bronx, your car won't start,
Your cell phone's dead, you can't call Triple-A,
And your mother's voice keeps saying "Now that wasn't
    very smart…"

I Can Resist Anything

Just swipe your card and you'll be entertained.
The preview's almost over. Do it now.
Enjoy it all, my love, until you're drained.

Your day was long. You fought, you lost or gained.
At last it's time for what days don't allow.
Just swipe your card and you'll be entertained.

Why are you waiting? Why have you refrained?
It's not as though you're too young to know how.
Enjoy it all, indulge until you're drained.

It's beautiful, this hour you've disdained,
More perfect than that thought creasing your brow.
Just swipe your card and you'll be entertained.

Drink up. Forget what you have not attained.
This life is short and hard. Don't you think so?
Enjoy it all, right now, until you're drained.

You have been told, you have been taught and trained,
But darling, that was then and this is now.
Just swipe your card and you'll be entertained.
Enjoy it all, my love, until you're drained.

Returning from a Vacation Cut Short by Political Turmoil

He had a heart attack and died.
They took his body off the plane.
No friend or lover by his side,
He had a heart attack and died
Where no one knew him. No one cried.
As we escaped that land of pain,
He had a heart attack and died.
They took his body off the plane.

Hydrogen Bomb Ignition Sequence

So now you've learned to make the flash with no known tense,
Which, falling into time, then made each grain of sand.
Strange, how it is a chain of diamond-cut events:
First, cock and pull cold Pluto's A-bomb trigger and
Ka-Pow! It smoothly crushes the next stage's sphere,
Igniting Tritium, Deuterium to equal
Four Helium, one neutron and…well, looky here:
A real-time, hot-damn thermonuclear blast sequel,
17.6 million electron volts
Of free, indifferent energy, a boiling blaze
Whose model is the old beginning force that jolts
Two atoms into one and yields the perfect rage
For order, radiation coupling x-ray dense.
Good job, my small, forked sparkplug! Nothing will be spared.
Come on, just one more time: $E = mc^2$.

The Demon Speaks of the Bottom Line

The world is cold and business deals go sour
All the time. I wish it weren't so hard,
But sweetheart, time is money, every hour,
And when it comes to time there's no trump card.
So the bottom line is what I'm looking for.
The bottom line is what I'd like to see:
Red ink or black, champagne or auditor?
And listen, what's in all of this for me?
For things might turn out fine, but often don't.
So I say: watch your back and make your luck.
And don't expect folks to be nice. They won't.
They'll fuck you if it's you they need to fuck.
Does this sound mean? Or heartless? Look at your life.
Show me the money. I'll show you the knife.

Lower Your Expectations

One problem is that you expect too much,
Like certain families from their vacations,
Or certain coaches from teams in the clutch.
Don't be a fool. Lower your expectations.
Regard the weatherman with skepticism.
Remember money is, for many, God.
Think of your family as a shattered prism
At best, at worst a clumsy firing squad.
Lower the bar for luck and health and friends,
For manners, honesty and dialogue.
Don't count on anyone to make amends.
Lower your expectations for your dog.
Put all those hopes up on some dusty shelf.
Especially the ones about yourself.

III. Kissing for Cynics

Impossible to Eat

The lemon hung high on the lemon tree.
I climbed up, grabbed it, plucked it and it spoke.
"Listen, stupid," it said, "you kiss me,
It's gonna hurt. I'm better in a Coke.
With rum. In beer. Or squirted on a fish.
Or mixed with sugar, in moist sponge cake, mousse.
My bitter peel, on an espresso dish
Or candied like a fossil, can seduce.
But you eat me direct, I promise pain.
It's not like you're some little kid whose tongue
Still hasn't touched the sour sorrow vein.
You're a grown man. Don't pretend you're young."
We hung there, we two, in that sweet fall breeze.
I bit, spat rind, then sucked and gave a squeeze.

When the Wind and Dark Waves Come

i.

Be angry when the wind and dark waves come.
Be angry in the inhuman house of stone.
Be angry though you still will be alone.
Be angry even if it strikes you dumb.

Let that arc be your dream among the trees.
Let it be the underlying song.
Let it be a fiction, but not wrong,
A lie that shines with possibilities.

Your time grows shorter as you read these letters.
The sun is throwing shadows down the floor.
Even oceans crack beneath time's thumb.
Yet here's a choice, within relentless fetters:
Lie down quietly forever, or
Be angry when the wind and dark waves come.

ii.
Be gentle when the wind and dark waves come.
Be gentle in the inhuman house of stone.
Be gentle though you still will be alone.
Be gentle even if it strikes you dumb.

Let that arc be your dream among the trees.
Let it be the underlying song.
Let it be a fiction, but not wrong,
A lie that shines with possibilities.

Your time grows shorter as you read these letters.
The sun is throwing shadows down the floor.
Even oceans crack beneath time's thumb.
Yet here's a choice, within relentless fetters:
Deny each other and the bad world, or
Be gentle when the wind and dark waves come.

What You Carry

i.

At the heart of heartbreak we find the heart
Of love. At the beating center of an anger
Anger must come second, cannot start
Without at first and always the fine heart's danger.
And at the burning core of grief we find that grief
Must be effect, not cause. Love must come first
For only love, however delicate and brief,
Can call and answer grief's relentless thirst.
So feel it, feel the pain but always know
However big pain is, pain is a shade.
Grief, heartbreak, anger, hate, each can but show
Itself, despite its strength, a mere charade.
Sorrow? It will come. But the love we make,
Though it embolden grief, grief cannot take.

ii.

Before the day the heart breaks comes the art
Of love. And in the furnace of an anger,
Remember anger burns but cannot start
Without the fuel: what's loved and is in danger.
And in that arid school study how grief
Must be effect, not cause. Love has come first,
For only love, though delicate and brief,
Can teach us that its absence is a thirst.
So feel it, feel the pain. Let yourself know
Heartbreak and anger, grief and what you carry.
It's real, it's there, it hurts and will not go
Because you tell it it is secondary.
And yet it is. Make love, and the love you make,
Though it will come to grief, grief cannot take.

Curses and Blessings

Let anger gnaw the world. Let rage run free.
Let snipers meditate upon your town.
Let microbes take your leg above the knee.
Let your children die in wars. No…let them drown.
May greed consume your day and lust your night,
Your home ignite with hatred and with strife.
May you at last agree that might makes right,
And understand the logic of the knife.

Then let spring come and show what it can do.
Let iron be reformed by flowering vines.
Let April be a sentence we construe.
Let flowers blossom in the mouths of mines.
And then, all curses turned but partly true,
Do more: imagine me, imagine you.

Analogue Redux

The simulacra multiply like rabbits,
No, frogs, no, dogs, although that's all ways wrong,
Because our unsexed nowhere pixel habits
Can't stick the quick real tangent to cool song.
Now music comes from ear buds, script from screens,
Friends from a million anonymities,
Theater from moments that were never scenes,
And even food courts unrealities.
I've got analogue nostalgia…but
I also dig my phone, my in-box panics
Of zap-stuffed ear plus eyeball brain-smack glut.
And times I need a break, there's always Xanax.
Yet darling, I wrote this by hand, where you could let it,
If you want less, arrive. Come and get it.

Kissing for Cynics

I saw them kissing in the lunch-hour street,
Indifferent to its big crowd on the fly.
She'd dropped her leather briefcase at her feet,
And he was dressed for work, nice suit, blue tie.
Could have been their first kiss or their last,
Fruit of love or where love starts to grow.
Maybe it was their future and their past —
No one who was there will ever know.
And yet big joy transpired in what they dared.
The way each chose. I saw it with my eyes.
For when he deeply kissed her, unprepared
She paused, but then embraced that sweet surprise.
Surrender, friend. Give in. It's never, ever over.
This world — your world — is always waiting for a lover.

A Prayer

Dear God: please kill me now and bring me back
A dancer, good one, pro who knows his stuff.
I say strike me down, I've had enough
Of poetry, its lassitude and lack
Of muscle burn and beauty's heart attack.
Here, make my flesh a dying world but buff
Enough to turn and jump like nothing, rough
Enough for every lift and fish dive. Smack
My back back into limber art and give me
Passion, grace and fire, perfect running,
High, low, hip-hop, ballroom, ballet, don't care.
I'll take the bloody feet, just let dance live me.
I've had enough of all this stupid punning.
Come on, you're God! I'm jumping. Are you there?

Tuesday, 9:11 A.M.

I look at you and need to know
How could you write what you did.
Foolish girl, silly girl, idiot —
"I keep my ideals, because in spite of everything
I still believe that people are really good at heart."
What nonsense.
O my cute little jackass in a frock, you've been betrayed.
The storm troopers are on the stairs and coming up.

Yet there you sit, smiling, refuting me, a ghost
Challenging every bitterness. Shown up by a stubborn little girl.
Forgive me, Anne. Perhaps I was wrong. And so I too will not
     surrender,
Not to my own heart breaking, nor to any greater ugliness,
     not even to whatever I may know that you do not,
     such as the day of your death, witness this haunting.

But let this not be a prayer. Let it be a promise
To ponder what you wrote.

The Poetry of Power

Bring it on, the poetry of power,
Art equal to the empire we've become.
Forget your self, that dewy, inward flower —
The markets' roar has rendered that world dumb.
Think big. Sunlit piazzas will not do —
Silver jets are blasting off the deck,
While instantaneous time is coming true.
It's not enough to rubberneck the wreck.
If I want that I'll turn on my TV.
No — stop, turn and face the greenhouse thunder.
We have to re-imagine liberty
In such a world, so full of quantum wonder,
Or we'll be ruled by genome, web and bomb.
So, citizen, come! And hold them in your palm.

To the Silence

A hard day, filled with silence. Not a word.
No "hello" and no "goodbye." No
"Come on," no "Go away," no swift bluebird,
Half-glimpsed as it arcs up, decides to go,
Leaving at least a quick pastel impression.
No "yes," no "no," no "maybe," and no gift,
No song, no question, thank-you or digression.
No lightning strike, no continental drift.
So this is love. It also is. Must be.
An emptiness from which no sense can come.
I'll go and measure it against the sea,
Because that way one cannot find a sum.
And though I've heard no word, I'll write, I will.
Listen: the waves, forever. I love you still.

Of Truth

The demon! Bastard! After me again!
This time he's chasing me with a pointed stick.
Blind alley. Trapped. He says "Remember when...?"
Advances, puts the point against my neck,
"Young and naïve, you thought and acted as,
Well..." he sneers, "young people do? As if
The truth were a kind of diamond Alcatraz,
An inescapable Chateau d'If?"
"Sorry, your honor," I say, "Can't recall."
"Bullshit!" he snarls, and presses. One drop, red.
He says "That hurt? Those sentences are all
Commuted. Money's gone to truth's dull head."
I pause. "Good point," I say. "True, ours is a dishonest age."
Too late, he apprehends his error. Exit, howling with rage.

A Flaw

"That's a flaw," she said. Straight to my face,
So close, like a slap, and true, so true it hurt.
"No, a mistake," I said, my wall in place,
As if that lie could make the truth divert.
Yet with the pain of that there came strange strength
From looking hard at what her careful thought
Illuminated through my whole life's length.
And in her steady gaze the blunt words brought
More good than what their simple sense could mean.
So later I could say, "Maybe the kind
Of thing that happened to you young no one
Gets over, ever. Maybe the trick's to find
Not strength but giving, knowing done is done."
So tangled in sweet uncounted hours we,
Mud mixed with wonder, studied intimacy.

A Conversation

"Come on — immortal? Is that a joke or a lie?
Hard drives go obsolete and print decays,
Memories all fade and lovers die,
Even the sun will die, and only fools count days.
Feel that? I'm real. So baby, please calm down.
If you love me, render me ephemeral.
Give me our now and not some future crown.
I want to be your lover, not your emerald.
Then if you must, when love has stripped us bare,
Just sketch me like the artists do whose pads
I litter, fleeting. For true love doesn't care
For dead rewards, your Odysseys and Iliads.
Perfection is so boring. Life is better.
Turn that thing off and run your fingers through my hair."

O Captain

Pulled up, cradled my sandy lance, ate lunch.
Mid-day, hot and quiet. Had an itch —
Standard issue boxers in a bunch —
But scratching under these clothes? Life's a bitch.
Sancho was complaining, pointed out
How our rides need up-armoring, ignored.
I nodded, ate my rations, said "No doubt."
Told him "Off-shift. Take a nap." He snored,
Then woke up, muttered "How about a beer?"
I laughed and closed my visor. A truck exploded
In the market, killing twenty. Fear,
Blood everywhere. We went in locked and loaded.
That's when all hell broke loose. I still believe.
I'm just so sorry that I had to leave.

A Student Applying to Med School
Comes to the Writing Center

Just to be within two feet of her
Dark eyes, her olive skin, black curling hair
Fresh from the shower, that lovely smile, the sure
Clear way she spoke about the care
That she could not provide her dad when he
Was suffering from ulcers, and her friend,
Who's had four tumors in her brain, made me
Wish that our hour together would never end.
Bilingual in Gujarati, smart as hell
And as beautiful as a pomegranate,
She brought her essay in, asked me to tell
Her how to say she wants to heal the planet.
Well...I did my best. But did she see?
To be within two feet of her helped me.

Fighting Back

The demon came to me again last night.
He woke me up and said "We have to talk."
I said "Not now," but he turned on the light,
Smiled, pulled a gun, said "Let's go for a walk."
"Cold?" he asked. "I'm naked," I replied,
"What do you think?" He laughed. Gave me his coat.
We were standing in a park. "They lied,"
He said, "The ones who told you you can float
Above my charms. You're flesh. So rest assured:
Hate, greed, megalomania and death
Rule every day and govern every word.
Someone profits from every child's first breath.
Now sleep on that." He vanished. Fire and smoke.
Dramatic bastard. Want to hear a joke?

Resurrection of a Mouse

What full, sad sounds the noise that you were making,
Clenched in our cat's jaws, pierced by a tooth,
Inevitably caught forever shaking
And squeaking, like a man who's seen the truth.
Sneaky pest who shat all over tables,
Vermin, host to rabies, hanta, louse,
I'm undeceived by all the mousy fables.
I'm glad you're gone. I'm pleased our cat can mouse.
Still I cannot forget your little death,
Prey to the satisfied play of calico.
Last night I dreamed I heard your last small breath
Bring life as far as any voice can go.
What more could any song be asked to bring?
Beyond all praise and blame, you chant, you sing.

The Great Redtail

The great redtail looked neither proud nor fierce
But rather clumsy in his lumbering retreat
As three small, black birds harried him across the sky,
Disturbing his soaring, diving on their enemy,
Who could not turn quickly enough to fend them off,
His talons useless, beak unable to respond to their tiny violences.
Now, my wrathful poet, what about this?
The implacable arrogance driven off this time,
Although he will return, dropping out of the sky like
    death itself —
Yet consider the tiny, brave songbirds, equally wild,
Demanding to be heard in their defiant joy,
Driving their attacker away from the trees and up into more
    rarified air,
Until, briefly free again from his terrible, remorseless eyes,
They can return to their lovely and peaceful nests in the cool
    of the evening.

Young Doctors in Love

A cold night in the middle of December.
We order beers, we shoot some pool. Sawdust.
They're holding hands. He says "I can't remember
How many dying people I've asked to trust
Me when I told them they'd be fine." She nods,
"There isn't any hope most of the time,
But if you tell them that, they think the gods
Can find some techno-cure. It's sad, a crime.
The family just buries itself in debt,
The patient dies." "The choices aren't real good ones,"
He says, "I think maybe we ought to let
More people die in quiet, as they could once."
Another round. Life suddenly so sweet.
We pay and head out, laughing in the street.

Young Poets in Their Obscurities

Young poets in their obscurities do not
Imagine how, when they grow older, they
May reach, arrive at, stumble on, be brought
To places where they know just what to say.
Some never get there, but for those who do,
The gate creaks open and the vines give way,
The brambles snap, and suddenly what's true
Stands like a courtyard nude in the light of day.
It's tempting to blurt out "You call this good?
It's old and obvious and so constrained…"
It's tempting to go back to the dense, dark wood
Where little can be seen and less explained.
Tempting. But there you are. Whatever you do,
The silent statue turns and looks at you.

I'm Yours

"Me?" I said, "Oh, I don't. Never could.
I mean, sometimes, to rock and roll, alone,
But, you know, this formal stuff? No good.
Besides, my friends want to go. It's almost one."
Excuses, jokes, no dice. The band was tired,
But still playing. A good friend's wedding night.
I'd met her over drinks. And now, inspired
By god knows what, she thought the time was right.
She said "Come on already. Those guys are bores.
I can get you past your clumsy walking.
Dave, you're going to sail across these floors.
Come on, take my hand. No more talking.
Just one short dance. We're here, so why not now?
You can dance. I'm yours. I'll show you how."

Get Tough

I'm sick of people dying. I've had enough.
The way they keep on dropping off is rude.
So I say let's live large. Go big. Get tough.

Enough of this relentless sorrow stuff.
Think positive. Work out. Eat more soul food.
I'm sick of people dying. I've had enough.

Love is our home. So let death huff and puff.
This little piggy's not going to come unglued.
And I say let's live large. Go big. Get tough.

Let's stoke our days so full no fact can snuff
A single quark out of beatitude.
I'm sick of people dying. I've had enough.

I think it's time we played a little rough.
I think it's time we got a little lewd.
So I say let's live large. Go big. Get tough.

Come on, folks. No more whining. No more fluff.
I want to see some serious attitude.
I'm sick of people dying. I've had enough.
So I say let's live large. Go big. Get tough.

Three Variations on a Theme by Wallace Stevens

Ramon Fernandez, tell me, if you know,
Why, when the singing ended and we turned
Toward the town, tell why the glassy lights,
The lights in the fishing boats at anchor there,
As the night descended, tilting in the air,
Mastered the night and portioned out the sea,
Fixing emblazoned zones and fiery poles,
Arranging, deepening, enchanting night?

i. Ramon's Reply

I met him at the bar, laughing, drunk,
A sparkle, but in a way reserved and shy.
We strolled, cigars and talk, then quiet. A funk?
Well, we're all entitled. I didn't pry.
Then we saw Carina on the beach.
As beautiful as ever. I love her so.
I wanted…but so much is beyond our reach.
The night came down and so we turned to go.
When I read his poem I thought, yes,
Her voice is one of the best I've ever heard.
It touched me too, it always does, I guess,
But not because of some mysterious word.
No, Wallace, the gulf is not so wide or wild.
She was my mistress, and carrying my child.

ii. Carina's Song

Men — what do they know? They make me laugh.
But not in anger — no. It's the way they seem
So lost so often, as if they're just half

Of what they are until they love a dream.
And why should I not be a lovely dream
To some of them? I find it fascinating.
Call me that name, but things aren't what they seem.
Yes, I'm untrue — but isn't all creating?
Ramon was filled with what he couldn't say —
Who knows why. I gave myself to him
Because I wanted to. His lucky day.
And now he worries this child belongs to him.
Perhaps it does. But who's that with Ramon?
Ah…he denies me. Well. I'll sing alone.

iii. A Child

I float within the genius of her sea.
Nothing forms to my voice; I have none.
I swim an ocean that was made for me,
Just as within me grows another one.
Sometimes the ocean sings. Soon so will I,
Not by chance but alive, water and song
Both vital, true, our spirit's constant cry.
Within this medleyed music I belong.
Don't tell me this sweet salt is meaningless.
It is my home. There is no other voice.
No greater order exists, no loneliness.
I am and love the world — I have no choice.
And more than I can say, I know my mother, maker,
Makes ocean song, song ocean. And I will not forsake her.

The Choreographer Auditions the Men

Knowing everything, the demon stood
At the *barre* and smiled and lashed his pointed tail.
Relaxed back straight, *demi pliés* so good,
Oh, good. *Grand pliés* she couldn't assail.
Liquid gold *tendus*, then *dégagés*,
Each *rond de jambe* perfection in its part.
A textbook *fondu* next, and then *frappés*,
Remarkable, as if cut with diamond art.
"Move like a blaze of consciousness," she said,
"Imperfect as we are," and now he frowned.
"*Tour jeté, passé, passé*," she said,
"*Arabesque! penché*!" He fell to the ground.
Gathered up his things. Glowered. Limped away,
"Embrace sweet gravity…" last words he heard her say.

In My Garden

Down on my hands and knees I plant. Descend,
Become a woman, touch me, take my hand,
Let things be what they might be, not pretend,
Not merely something I can understand.
Whether in parking lot or on some mountain,
Let the moment come to kiss your lips
Or carry you through a deserted fountain,
Defying every day's dictatorships.
For all this dirt is like an epitaph
That on its own remembers how to sing.
That's why the moment that I hear you laugh
I bend to work at our continuing.
Your eyes, your slender back with its tattoo —
It's May. I call your name. I call to you.

Odd Words

Whatever happens is just what it is.
It is not something else, it cannot be
What it is not, now can it? No, it's this
And only this this single thing can be.
Each thing alone can only sing and bring
Itself, so learn the taste of desolation.
Give in, give up, give out and let each thing
Go down the path it must out of creation…
Unless the sun give one look, that look give
Us day then night, that night join dusk and dawn
To us, and that time, two times, we two live
Each vital minute redux, tender, gone…
But that's more difficult than syntax and why would
Even words agree to such subjunctive good?

The Old Pain

Ah, the old pain, yes, always the best.
He strolls in like a friend, draws up a chair.
The old familiar feeling in your breast,
Cool knowledge that the visits never end.
No formal feeling here, you share a drink.
It's not like you just met, you're on good terms.
In the aftermath of grief he lets you think,
Look back in love or anger or regret.
You rage no more about what is or was.
He's silent, knows his way around the house.
This is his gift to you, this calm because,
This moment where there's nothing left to say.
It's not that bad, this life. At least it's true.
You look him in the eye. He looks like you.

Many Poets and Critics Now Distrust Coherence, Stylistic Finish and Closure Because, They Argue, They Contradict the Experience of Modern Life

Everything changes, except the avant-garde. Valéry

Now what a day it's been, another bout
Filled with such sweet surprises. First, a friend
Asked in an email if I'd heard about
The New York City hit-and-run that brought an end
To a mutual friend's ex-husband's life. So long:
Two kids. And then, out of the blue, a call
To say the survey of our home is wrong:
"Hey neighbor, and that old retaining wall?
It's gone." Now number three: a nice long swim,
A peaceful pool, late summer sun, relief.
A former student, lifeguard, seems to brim
With life, gives me a hug, then sobs with grief.
Cancer's done to her aunt what cancer does.
And your point about the sonnet was...?

Dead Flies

Seven drowned flies in a white wine glass,
A crisp September morning, slanting light.
I left it on a counter overnight
And sugar wrought *in vino veritas.*
No — one still feebly flaps a wing as if
There's some escape. The others all are dead.
This is what happens if you lose your head,
Seduced by such a deep *apéritif.*
That's what I'm thinking as I pour then flush
Their alcohol-soaked carcasses away.
But I can see the other side as well:
Midnight, hunger, sweetness and a rush
Of irresistible desire no thought can quell.
There are worse ways to go. Whaddayasay?

Freed in the Act

"Tell me," he said, "if you read all of that,
What would you know that you do not know now?
Where would you be that you are not now at?
What could you do that now you don't know how?"
He paused to let the words sink in, then said,
"Can any sentence bring him back to life?
Can you write something that will raise the dead?
All your words do is document the knife."
I wish you could have seen his face when I
First greeted him then cursed, yelled "No!" and "Yes!"
Then made a promise followed by a lie.
I swore an oath, then vowed I would confess,
Congratulated him then called him names.
He's gone. I guess he didn't like these games.

To Failure

O Failure, dog and dirty, crack and rust,
Black rot, cracked heart, burnt, broken words gone numb,
Dumb blunt sum of every twisted trust,
Sorrow's ash, sad silence, bad hip: come!
Make every paradise a filthy slum.
Spread your stain like promises gone bust.
Drive me home in darkness, screw your thumb
Into my tongue and write jokes in the dust.
Just remember: every time you speak
You're speaking here, and every time you win
You yourself extend a winning streak.
No rest. It must get tiring. Dawn: Begin.
Come trip me up, make every good thing end,
Yes, without fail. Fool, you are my friend.

At a Party

i. A Poorly Understood Process

The first step in a star's birth is to wait.
In time some shock runs through a cloud of stuff.
Next, if chance tweaks ripples to a rate
Of angular momentum swift enough,
And given sufficient mass of swirling dust
Accruing over eons they swing tight,
One day, obscure and cold no more, all must
Shed their opacity, fuse, and ignite.
Then no dim protostar ambiguous,
But a hydrostatic equilibrium
Explosion furnace, 18 million plus,
It boils and burns, its parts less than its sum.
How now, my warm, sweet speck! We're made from that.
   Come, let's aspire
To cinch our own dark orbit home and burst back into fire.

ii. Obvious Bullshit

Oh, thank-you for that little science class.
I learned so much about so much from it.
It's quite a lovely way to make a pass,
Even if it's obvious bullshit.
I have to admire the way you thought to evade
The fallacy of saying we're like stars.
It's good, I get it — not like them but made
From what they make, their elements now ours.
But she's not hot enough, your muse of fire —

The problem lies in your appeal to law.
Although I know my own pangs of desire,
I'm not their slave and that's your case's flaw.
Gravity's fine, but I obey its spirit, not its letter.
No – before I take off even this soft sweater,
You're simply going to have to get to know me better.

Quigley Writes

"All this doing is finally itself
The problem." Bearded Buddha, I agree.
The wise course: stack the cities on a shelf
Labeled *Politics* or *History*.
This world's on fire and always has been burning.
Everything we do just turns out wrong
And nothing quells the ancient, bloody yearning.
How foolish, thinking we could mend that song,
Except perhaps in a private, glowing garden.
The old dream: mountainside above the sea,
Where long ago the lava slowed to harden.
Green is the order of the day and free.
Remnants of the rainbow fill the mind.
And the only native snake found here is blind.

After the Anger

After the anger has burned itself away,
After every expensive mistake,
After you've cracked a knuckle on the day,

After rectitude has had its way,
Like a thirst that only rage can slake —
After the anger has burned itself away,

After the final scene in the one-act play
Of words and words, their long heartache —
After you've cracked a knuckle on the day,

After you have forgotten how to pray,
For you have watched your own heart break —
After the anger has burned itself away,

After October has succeeded May
And handed you a broken rake —
After you've cracked a knuckle on the day,

Like stone and star, with nothing left to say,
Imperfect angel, then let it be love you make
After the anger has burned itself away,
After you've cracked a knuckle on the day.

Before the Fact

The raised voice, table smack, demands, door slammed.
Such fearful rattling of the body's cage.
The ugly way the day goes down now damned…
Some call it anger but in fact it's rage.
For rage is action. Rage requires hands
And eyes and all words to surrender to
Its pure prerogative, diamond demands
That only it and nothing else be true.
Note how, in contrast, anger is not feral,
Just an emotion, not the realized act.
It need not in and of itself cause peril.
It offers up a choice before the fact.
Anger? Anger's fine. Tell me of yours.
I'll tell you mine. We'll talk. Unlock the doors.

Whistling in January

The ice inside the window seems forever.
Transmission fluid slows to tired glue.
At dusk the sky gives up its weak, thin blue.
Blue stars shine off the mercury at never.
The earth obeys its dark, tremendous lever.
The skating on the lake is fast and true.
Dogs whine, limp, bite their paws, and call to you.
Things stiffen, harden, halt, stop, break, and sever.
But larger than its hour and more than ice,
Beyond its temporary shape and end,
Only itself, away from which it's slipping,
Time passing and arriving at a price
That's still a moving sign of how we'd bend:
One icicle in the new sun, slowly dripping.

Apalhraun and Helluhraun

I dreamed again of Iceland, dazzling island
Of driven clouds, volcanic fissures, fish.
I've never been, but when...give me a while and
I'll wish us up things glacier bursts might wish.
I'll learn the language, study every curve
Of coastline, every gray-green eye, devise
A life in love no lava can unnerve —
Then take my own advice and end my lies.
In Iceland cold waves march and breach
Forever on black sand, sea birds ascend
And call and settle back upon the beach.
How I wish this dream would never end.
Midnight. The streets are quiet. No one fights.
The glaciers crawl. Look up: the northern lights.

Address to the Expository Sparrow

Enough already with the explanations.
I've climbed the ladder to your messy nest,
Studied accounts of your wide emigrations.
Don't need to hear again which seeds taste best.
Spare me the lecture on your trembling claws,
Your history of war with the chickadee.
I know you, like the mouse, have learned our laws,
You antagonistic refugee.
No, *Passer Domesticus*, don't give
Me any of your uric acid crap.
Hoodlum, gangster, rat of the air, you live
Like us, against all odds, all over the map.
I'm here to say: remember the hawk's dark wing.
Come on, you little bastard: Sing, sing. Sing!

These Long Years On

Where did they go, the sorrow and the pain?
God knows, they're tough enough and don't give in.
Why should they? They have everything to gain.
They know that in the end they're going to win.
Yet in this moment, trying to begin,
There are words words cannot begin to say.
And look: the sorrow and the pain give way,

Give way, dissolve like rain, and on the long
Drive home, the wind blowing and raking dark
Years and loneliness, a lonely song
Playing on the radio, a spark
Here and there in the sky making its mark,
I wonder where the two of them have gone,
For now, the sorrow and the pain, these long years on.

Ivangorod, Ukraine, 1942

*This is the treason of the artist: a refusal to admit the
banality of evil and the terrible boredom of pain...But to
praise despair is to condemn delight, to embrace violence is
to lose hold of everything else.*   Ursula K. Le Guin

Upon a windswept field the color of lead,
A woman holds her child against her breast.
A soldier aims his rifle at her head.

A field and photograph her only bed,
She turns her humble back and does her best
Upon a windswept field the color of lead,

Where she endures, forever, final dread.
The shutter clicks. The moment has confessed:
A soldier aims his rifle at her head.

Why are we here? Why do we eat this bread?
Why does time give this agonizing test
Upon a windswept field the color of lead?

For now this field, where she and her child bled,
Though just a field, disturbs my work and rest:
A soldier aims his rifle at her head.

Yet, murdered woman who cannot be unsaid,
I hear the small, brave words with which you blessed.
Here on a windswept field the color of lead,
A soldier aims his rifle at your head:

Hold on. I love you. Do not be afraid.

Out, Bitterness, Out

Out, bitterness, and take your goddamn apple
With its worm. Sourpuss, this is your pill,
And don't forget your line and rusting grapple,
The one you used to hook my windowsill.
Here's your icicle, your sprig of cress,
Your almond, aloe, root, all cut in two.
We no longer share the same address.
Your truth is not the only thing that's true.
I'll admit that you once soothed my eyes,
A roommate sympathetic to my sorrow.
But I'm alive and you don't compromise.
You've overdrawn our past. Now it's tomorrow.
I've learned my lesson: I am filled with doubt.
But that means scruples for you. Come on, get out!

IV. BRING IT

True Love

It was an imperfection but it was
So perfect, in the way the ocean strives
Imperfectly to do what ocean does.
It was an imperfection but it was
Almost perfect, although, perhaps because
It was imperfect it fulfilled our lives.
It was an imperfection but it was
So perfect, in the way the ocean strives.

Catch

Both of us boys who loved to throw it hard
Back then when we were boys, and having argued
Over stupid things, we stood too far
Apart to talk in Colorado sunshine
And made that dirty ball fly like a word
In silence, back and forth, the only sound
Resounding, satisfying smacks of glove
Sting at connection when the catch locked in,
And playing there we did the only dance
Worth doing, with our hands, our eyes, our feet
And each best guess acquired long ago
For this: to send a hardball sailing up
And out as question, message, exclamation,
The very moment of sweet conversation.

Eschew Obfuscation

I love you and will love you until all
The dimwits change their clearly confused minds,
Until the astronomically small
Becomes a little big beneath calm winds,
Until, against the even odds, one size fits all.

I'll love you until all the clever fools,
Those sophomores, catch on, which they will not,
For our failsafe, discretionary rules
Will prove foolproof when put to spoken thought,
Unleashing real magic in all home schools.

I'll love you until everything makes sense,
Until paid volunteers say "Problem solved"
With sure-bet resolute ambivalence.
So go ahead, back up. It's a true, solved
Mystery, an eloquent silence,

But I'll love you through each bright night, dark day,
Even if I don't know what to say.

1963: The Man with the Monkey

Stands before our home in Santiago,
Smiles, never says a word. Beneath great trees,
He grinds out liquid sparks, stirs a farrago
Of sweet incomprehensibilities.
His thin clothes hang, his right hand cranks the organ
Slowly, while to my new brother monkey
I laugh and sing and call out "More! Again!"
He dances up his master's back to the clunky
Box on the pole, receives my proffered orange,
Then sits there eating, leashed, green fez, green vest,
And takes me in. Creaking like a door hinge,
The moment opens, offering its test
Of what a day can be. Music pours from wood.
The monkey eats. The old man cranks. It is so good.

890 Square Feet of Reality

You gotta see this guy. His name is Tom.
More than twenty years short-order cook.
Don't know his last name, don't know where he's from.
He cooks so fast he barely needs to look:
Two rafts of hash brown smoothed out on the griddle,
Three Teflon pans, two eggs in each, then out,
Quick flip, spray oil, check hash, scrape smooth, talk little,
Cut hash, build plates, load perfect toast. No doubt.
A meal a minute, so efficient he
Can take his time, lean back, arms crossed, surveying
The clientele, his work gives symmetry
To need — the way a god might answer praying.
Let there be breakfast! Now Fiona brings
A number three. Sunrise: the radio sings.

Vox Balaenae

That December, snarled in crab pot lines
Off San Francisco near the Farallones,
The humpback cow began to drown, our tiny vines
Unyielding to her quiet overtones.
Done in by Munchkins, ropes wrapped tight around tail
And back and left front flipper, could she know
To mourn the long migration that would fail,
Crying, "O let me go to Baja, let me go"?
Can't say. But as the divers cut her free,
The long ropes dropping away, she lay at rest
And watched them work until, in liberty
Before departing, she swam up abreast
In turn to each as if to say goodbye,
Regarding each with her enormous eye.
And then she turned, swam in a growing circle,
Chose her course, breathed deep, and sounded for home.

Noah in Paradise

My Noah, 3, runs blond and savage, pisses,
Cries and laughs whenever he damn chooses,
Loves frogs and snails, to whom he offers kisses,
And knows no bounds to anger when he loses.
"Daddy, hold my hand," he says, then kicks
Me out of bed to sleep with mom and snore
Away exhaustion earned by throwing sticks
At waves and tumbling on the untamed shore.
Little Dionysus, free as fire,
Game-boy wonder, belly-laughter king,
At home upon the throne of wild empire,
Point your royal finger, yell "No," sing.
As long as you, your majesty, can rule,
I'll do my best to make the world your fool.

Please Is Asleep

"Please." A simple word, so hard to learn,
Long with acknowledgments that all imply
Each one of us is going to get a turn.
And Noah, five, why should he even try —
Since thirst burns so immediate in youth —
Enunciating that complexity?
"I need more milk in my cup!" was his great truth,
So he said that, instead of "please," to me.
And as his father, I of course said "Now,
Son, what's so hard about the small word 'Please?'"
Long look. The shoulders hunch. A furrowed brow.
Every civil moment's on its knees,
Every king who's ever ruled begins to weep
Pure tears of joy as Noah says: "Please is asleep."

E

Noah is making letters. Well, one letter.
Out of chaos everything has changed.
Before, there wasn't any worse or better,
Just incoherent scribbles he arranged,
And when we asked he'd tell us "That's a cat!"
Or "It's a shark, a mad shark," or "That's you."
At which we'd nod and praise, say "Oh, a cat!"
Or talk of colors, for the cat was blue.
But then today he brought us a new page
Of seven spidery figures fully meant.
Big "E"s, small "E"s, "E"s in every stage.
I watched him make one, gentle, slow, intent.
Not by chance. "Look!" he says, "E! E!"
Why E? Don't know. But O, my son — you're free.

To Celebrate Noah's Achievement of 100% on a Spelling Test

Many people *import* the oddest freedom,
Always looking to pour a stupid *acid*
Where the novel *estate* of their own thinking
Might have risen above the *insect* droning
Life would have us believe is all our *plot* is.
Disregard that obtusest *angle*, Noah.
Listen! *Robins* are singing in the treetops!
Chilly evenings are ripening the apples.
Dusk is here, and these moments after sunset
Rumble slightly with *trucks* — it's still the rush hour.
See? Each word, in its opening, is an *exit*
From the *ultra*-seclusion that surrounds us.
Learn them, love them (and spell them right) and they will,
Now and then, if you're lucky, bring you wonder.

Earthbound

Singing and hovering to show his fitness,
The lark soared fifty feet above the plain.
He hung and sang and waited for a witness
To all his aspiration, bliss and pain.
In England there are only ten percent
The number of these birds that there were twenty
Years ago, because of the advent
Of autumn cereal planting, which makes plenty

Of cereal but makes it hard for the lark, which nests on
the ground, to find its food between the next summer's
mature stalks. But this is no doubt for the best, because,
after all, there's a planet to feed and there's still plenty of
seed for many other birds, such as the crows, which are
also content to eat roadkill. And here in the New World
there is still the western meadowlark, *sturnella neglecta*,
so named because it was confused with the eastern
meadowlark for years, although we now know it is a
distinct species that nests on the ground in open country
in western and central North America but is neglected
no more, serving as the state bird of Kansas, Montana,
North Dakota, Oregon and Wyoming, and why not, as,
standing golden chest puffed out each spring upon his
bragging post, the male makes warbling, watery, flute-
like calls.

He is not a voice within a cloud,
Does not ascend so high to sing. No king,

Or, lost in some bright sky-bound ring, too proud,
But instead a new world icterid, he descends to sing.
"One need not be invisible to be free,"
Sings meadowlark in earthbound ecstasy.

Her Meditation

She was walking barefoot through a field
Carrying a sack of home-made bricks,
All stamped with hard words, each one fired and sealed
With heat that even grief cannot unfix.
She poured them out where a hot-air balloon
Stood pegged down in the grass, the propane burning,
Its envelope primed like the sun at noon
To head for points indifferent to our yearning.
She lifted up each hard-earned stone and said
"Goodbye" and put it in the empty basket,
Then pulled the tethers free and laid her head
Back on the earth. Nothing more to ask it.
The ship rose up with such surprising ease.
The pain was gone. Out of the west, a breeze.

When Our Life

Lady, when our life is done,
When we're just two clods of dirt,
When a new, indifferent sun
Has bleached away this flesh, our shirt,
When wind and rain have gone to work with seeds
Reincarnating us as flowers and weeds,
Then I say let the dumb facts be forgotten.
Let them sink into what's rich and rotten.

Let's take a vow we just don't care
If folks remember what we did,
Let's promise not to kneel in prayer
Before some dull truth's pyramid.
For no thin record of our work and days
Will ever penetrate their past's thick haze,
No archive, video or monument
Reveal or prove where all our quick hours went.

No, in an age of stone cold data,
Transforming life to one and zero,
I'd rather be *persona non grata*
Than some dumb fifteen-minute hero
Who scholars, spies and journalists produce.
For fact is none of that will be of use
To show some fool what we were when we dreamed,
Knowing the world for far more than it seemed.

Darling, wouldn't it be more fun
If in some distant future study,

In his Preface or Chapter One
A puzzled sage wrote "It's all muddy.
Their lives, the poems teach us, brimmed and overflowed
With tender passion, love, vitality. They plowed
Through life on fire like a burning asteroid.
Too bad the records all have been destroyed.

"All we know beyond the work is
That they wore flowers in their hair,
That they ran off and joined the circus,
Learned to juggle, fly through the air.
The rest is stuff of legends, vibrant silence,
A thread of pleasure through the world's drab violence.
They seem to show up in surprising places,
But why? Who knows? All they've left is traces."

That's what they'll read while outside May
Is blossoming with warm consent,
White hawthorn petals floating away,
Sweet lilac spending yet unspent.
Besides, who'd want to hear about each chore,
Our aging and our dying? What a bore,
When here they'll always find love hot and sly,
My hand beneath your dress, yours in my fly.

What will always matter are,
Small and perfect, your white breasts,
More fine than apples with caviar,
Endlessly young beyond all tests
Right might seek to impose on this: that down,
When we make love, time's tomcat purrs, lies down
In sulking splendor by our bed to wait,
Noting how we stop to conjugate.

So let facts go, they'd just make folks depressed.
We lived and made some love, to hell with the rest.
It's mostly nonsense and we did our best.
And now the sun has played but been finessed.
It's time to grow older, to be unblessed.
Lady, shouldn't we be getting dressed?

The Place You Take

The place your swimming body takes in the sea
Is unimportant and the place you take
When walking late at night alone but unalarmed
Down deserted boulevards lined with royal palms
Or lying reading in bed and then asleep
Is passing and irrelevant to the quick
Of hovering gull and low-flying pelican line,
Of green-blue breakers riffled by wind, the wick
Of each day burning into blindness and the deep
Sea throwing down meditations that it then calms.
All ignore the charm of motion in the charmed,
Wide emptiness, the inconsequential wake,
The place your body, swimming, takes in the sea.

Volcano of Blossoms

Jungle everywhere. The cries of birds.
Green canopy that hides the sky from view.
The mountain always there, like something true
But dormant, a word awaiting other words.
Alone like every other living thing,
Tangled in vines above a simmering vent
That long ago all reason thought was spent,
It drowses like a toucan's folded wing.
But locals claim the earth still sometimes moves
The way their parents told them it once did.
And some say soon the cleft will show its powers
Again when the deep rift gives and, giving, proves
Death less than this voluptuous pyramid,
The sky awash with shuddering and flowers.

Prosecco

Arrived at dawn. The train from Nice all night.
The shops still dark. No boats. *Pensione* closed.
One open café in the glittering light.
So: backpacks at our feet, maps out and posed
To walk the city. Then big Olaf stopped
And laughed, said "Visiting?" in his red beard,
Paused, then "Come on, I'll show you around." We hopped
From church to church, although a bar appeared
Between each one. "This waiter is my friend,"
Olaf would say, as if it were his mission
To mix Giorgione with *Valdobiaddene*
And get not only drunk but drunk on Titian.
We stumbled to the Frari altar. Hear that laughter echo?
Love, bring the glasses, kiss me, pop the cork again: Prosecco.

Joy

He died two years ago, at seventeen,
My sweet-willed student, rising free-ski star.
He'd always landed switch-540s clean
But went too big this time and spun too far.
In college now, she babysits my boys.
The plastic band that bears his name is blue,
Hard evidence she's learned what time destroys.
I ask. "Just friends," she says. I sense it's true.
A pause. "But…you know…Here." Out on the stairs,
She looks me in the eye. Words overflow.
"… They did it on my couch." Cute friend of theirs.
A wistful smile. "I thought you'd want to know."
You funny, lanky, long-haired boisterous kid.
I'd thought you never….What joy to know you did.

Thy Name Is As Ointment Poured Forth

A party. Loud and awkward. Drinks. Caged birds.
Traffic down below on the dark freeway.
An eyebrow and a shoulder suggest words
He knows she wants or needs to but won't say.
"All right, let's go," he whispers, offers a kiss.
Home, "Dumb party," she says and he says "Why?"
She says "They're all so fake. What an abyss.
Everything I say feels like a lie
When I'm with them." They sleep. Dawn. The sun,
Rising, obeys them, made participant
In love's broken perception, the mind outdone
And cleaving to the facts of what it can't...can't...
Express. Even the right words don't sound right —
So much names each to the other's lonely night.

For a Wedding

True love is good enough in its own way,
But runs too metaphysical to prove
Sufficient in the growing day-by-day
Of marriage. For a blind and wild true love,
The kind that feeds on every little need,
Goes always grasping after what is pure.
Its insatiable desire must soon exceed
A common sense where things might be agreed.
That's why we turn from truth to what's more sure,
It's why a thriving marriage isn't "true" —
No, we call it "good," because it works.
And that's the greatest thing marriage can do,
A lot less neat, perhaps, but wise: it works.
You're married now, so my advice is: pull
Back from perfection. Give up that control,
Take the failures that might break your trust
And let them turn so far inferior
To what you promise here, they crumble into dust.
For failure cannot make the good heart poor.
Forgive. Forgive! Practice forgiving, full
Of knowledge. For hot truths grow resentful
Of flaws, but a good marriage knows much more.
True love? It's not enough. Go beyond and you'll
Make love in marriage good: more real, more beautiful.

Galatea to Pygmalion

Home from modeling.
I struck some poses with you in mind.
Nude propped on an elbow, admiring her lover.
One artist sketched my back —
I wanted to ask her for it, give it to you.
But what would you do with a drawing of my back?
The artists bring music and wine. They are courteous.
One insisted on silence so she could hear breathing,
The scratch of charcoal.
Another arrives straight from his construction job,
Carharts dirty, homemade easel of two by fours and plywood.
Ramón will graduate in a few weeks and head off somewhere,
June always stakes out the corner and quietly labors,
Tania brings plates to prepare for etchings.
I work to please them, laughing to myself
At the delicious difficulty of remaining still,
The chill of a draft, a drop of sweat.
They appreciate it, although they grumble
That I don't fit on their paper. Indeed not.

Oh darling, if they only knew how sweet
The feeling is as they labor to turn back into art
What the goddess made into life for us.
Their failures fill me with delight.
And my pulse quickens when I realize
That soon you will return and read these words,
The product of my living hand just minutes ago.
I imagine that smile of yours I love, so hopeful.

Come to me. I am upstairs,
Mortal, languorous, and more beautiful
Than even you can imagine,
Wearing only flowers in my hair.

A Synapse

If memories can haunt us it's because
They are in fact alive, prefontal cortex,
Hippocampus swimming without pause,
Amygdala and dentate gyrus a vortex
Of what we used to call the heart, that fire
In fact electric from one neuron axon
To the dendrite of another with desire
Forever burning where there's life, a klaxon
Clamoring almost inaudibly
To spark, to reach, to touch, to feel, to know
Young lovers, who somehow and suddenly
Now understanding, both decide to go,
Like the first time we kissed, your place beneath
That office. Oh, the parts young people try on.
Remember? I unzipped your jeans with my teeth,
And you made love like a tiger. No, a lion.

She Receives Flowers

"Late in life you don't expect romance.
You don't expect to be swept off your feet.
You don't expect to have another chance.
You've learned to take the bitter with the sweet.
You have reviewed each season and its cause,
The brilliant, wind-swept days, the driving rains.
You tell yourself that there are certain laws,
· That now only the harvest-time remains.
So what are you supposed to do, when feral
Leopards prowl your blood beneath the moon,
And roses, invitation spangled with peril,
Appear upon your doorstep after noon?"
Sweet friend, this is your door. He sent you flowers.
Surrender to this sight, this scent, these hours.

Elegy for a Breast

Darling, no doubt you loved it more than I.
After all, it was a part of you.
Yet when the doctors told you you might die,
You cried but said "OK," and they cut through.
And I am glad they did, for here you sit,
Smiling and alive, your glass half full,
Your laugh the same, that sweet sarcastic wit
Still sparkling like a star. I feel its pull.
And I remember how you laughed then said,
Pointing your finger, "Rothman…just…this…once."
Then took your blouse off, kneeling on my bed,
And let me kiss you, every inch and ounce.
It was…you were…well, I can't even start.
Your eyes. Your lips. My hand so near your heart.

All I Thought

It used to be that all I thought about.
And yet I felt that I would never find.
I'd sunk into a place where only doubt.
And when I contemplated how the blind.
Back then I felt that no change ever could.
I thought fulfillment was a feeling that.
It seemed a sorry fiction that a good.
I thought I had accepted I was at.
Then I met you and everything became.
And now the only thing I want to do.
Now every hour, although it takes the same.
And now I know that there can be a true.
These words themselves are evidence a door.
This world's alive, and you, by giving more.

Bring It

Bring it. Bring the sweetness and the pain,
And bring the dream achieved and dream deferred.
Recall saguaro deserts, mountain rain.

Acknowledge doubt but hear the one true word.
Charge us to love our choices yet love life.
Keep in mind at all times plow and sword.

Hide nothing but do not reveal the knife.
Undo what should not be, but not too fast.
Seek peace except where you must still seek strife.

Stand for the future but stand on the past.
Embrace the market, but not money changers.
Indulge the sirens but stay near the mast.

Now all around you crowd the hungry dangers,
On every side and surely deep within.
Be courteous, because they are not strangers,

And don't forget to drink a little gin.
Make haste! But slowly. And carefully explain,
As you have done. Here are our hands, again. Begin.

Goodbye

It wasn't that I chose. I had no choice.
The pain was just too much. And so I gave
The last thing that I had and in this voice,
These words, like this, I said to him "I love
You, I forgive you," and I cradled Night
And rocked him in my arms. Now he began
To weep, "Don't make me go back there…that light…
I have to leave some way I understand,"
But I said "You came here through me, and that
Is how you'll go," and kissed him tenderly
Right on the lips. He howled and smoked and spat
And clawed and fought, and called me enemy.
I held his hand. I said his name. Undone
Where all began, we melted into one.

On a Ridge of Arapahoe Peak

There it stood, stunned, stunted, ice-laced wind
Allowing full growth only in the lee
Of an erratic boulder. Above, fury
Bore down perfectly out of the north, blind
Sculptor blasting every single thing.
Engelmann Spruce *Krummholz*, whose tenacious
Sap ebbs and flows to show just how ferocious
Life meets infinity with a green wing,
Undistracted, fated treeline tree
Thriving wierdly, clutching the rich rock
High on Arapahoe's thin ridge, you break
Into oblivion's pledge to set time free
Forever in the void the darkness planned.
Whatever is is you and there you stand.

Bases Loaded, Down 3, Bottom of the 9th, 2 Out, 3 and 1

She stood there on the mound holding the ball
Behind her willowy back, nodded, then smiled.
She fired it in, I swung, then came the call:
"Strike two!" It hurt. The hometown fans went wild,
Apollo cheering in his golden box,
Dionysus with his garments rent,
Roaring "You suck!" and throwing fruit and rocks.
All my heroes dead, indifferent.
I waited seven years, she pitched again.
This time I saw it coming, low, inside,
Crouched down, stepped back, swung, felt the crack, and then
I got to watch that ball go for a ride.
It launched into the upper deck's abyss.
The crowd shut up. They hadn't expected this.
And fact is next time odds are good I'll miss.
But as I rounded third, she laughed and blew a kiss.

Acknowledgments

Grateful acknowledgment is made to the the following
journals, presses and organizations for permission to
reprint poems which originally appeared with them,
occasionally in earlier versions.

Journals

American Arts Quarterly Online: "This Bright Edge"
Appalachia: "Vox Balaenae"
The Barefoot Muse: "I I I I I," "Hair of the Dog"
Blue Unicorn: "On First Looking into a Trendy Literary
    Periodical"
Contemporary Sonnet: "The Demon Opens an Auction"
The Crested Butte Chronicle and Pilot: "Let It Snow,"
    "Whistling in January"
The Edge City Review: "Acting My Age"
The Gettysburg Review: "We All Got Up to Dance"
The Gunnison Valley Journal: "Joy," The Great Redtail"
Harvard Magazine: "The Place You Take"
The Hudson Review: "Ivangorod, Ukraine, 1942"
Jewish Quarterly (UK): "Fighting Back"
Light: "That Apple," "You Can't Dance to the News," "In
    Your Dreams"
The Lyric: "I'm Yours," "E"
Marginalia: "Dark Quantum Foam's Hereafter," "The
    Choreographer Auditions the Men"
Measure: "At a Party"
Nebo: "The Poetry of Power"

The New Formalist: "Hydrogen Bomb Ignition Sequence,"
  "O Captain"
Prism Quarterly: "The Question"
The Raintown Review: "When Our Life"
Sparrow: "Thy Name Is as Ointment Poured Forth"
Tar River Poetry: "Matins"
Think Journal: "Please Leave"
The Threepenny Review: "The Demon Speaks of the
  Bottom Line"

Books

The Geography of Hope: Poets of Colorado's Western Slope.
  Ed. David J. Rothman. Crested Butte, CO: Conundrum
  Press, 1998: "Youth," "When the Wind and
  Dark Waves Come," "Resurrection of a Mouse."
Hot Sonnets. Ed. Moira Egan and Clarinda Harris.
  Washington DC: Entasis Press, 2011: "She Receives
  Flowers," "Volcano of Blossoms."

Reprints

"Dark Quantum Foam's Hereafter," The Colorado Poets
  Association, http://www.coloradopoets.org/april9,
  courtesy of *Marginalia*.
"You Can't Dance to the News," Lighthouse Writers
  Workshop: AAP National Poem in Your Pocket Day,
  courtesy of *Light*.
"Bring It" appeared under the title "Yes We Can" on
  The Lighthouse Writers Blog on December 30, 2008.
  It is archived at:
  http://lighthousedenver.wordpress.com/?s=Rothman

Other Acknowledgments:

"The Question" won Honorable Mention in the
Dancing Galliard Sonnet Contest, 2007, which is sponsored
by *Prism Quarterly* /Daybreak Press.

"When the Wind and Dark Waves Come," "Curses and
Blessings," "After the Anger," "Youth," "Her Medita-
tion" and "Elegy for a Breast" served as the basis for a
ballet by Mark Godden, "Imagine Me, Imagine You."
This work was produced by Ballet Nouveau Colorado
and premiered at the Lakewood (CO) Cultural Center on
February 6, 2009.

Finally, I owe a great debt to my old friend Valerie Lester
for her invaluable reading of this manuscript. No one
could ask for a more thoughtful, precise, honest, skilled
and generous critic.